STAR WARS
Princess Leia's Adventures

Senior Editor Matt Jones
Project Art Editor Chris Gould
Designer Thelma-Jane Robb
US Senior Editor Jennette ElNaggar
Production Editor Marc Staples
Senior Production Controller Laura Andrews
Managing Editor Emma Grange
Managing Art Editor Vicky Short
Publisher Paula Regan
Art Director Charlotte Coulais
Managing Director Mark Searle

Reading Consultant Barbara Marinak

First American Edition, 2025
Published in the United States by DK Publishing,
a division of Penguin Random House LLC
1745 Broadway, 20th Floor, New York, NY 10019

Page design copyright © 2025 Dorling Kindersley Limited
25 26 27 28 29 10 9 8 7 6 5 4 3 2 1
001-345291-Feb/2025

© & TM 2025 LUCASFILM LTD.

All rights reserved.
Without limiting the rights under the copyright reserved above, no part of this publication may be reproduced, stored in or introduced into a retrieval system, or transmitted, in any form, or by any means (electronic, mechanical, photocopying, recording, or otherwise), without the prior written permission of the copyright owner.
Published in Great Britain by Dorling Kindersley Limited

A catalog record for this book
is available from the Library of Congress.
ISBN 978-0-5939-6203-9 (Paperback)
ISBN 978-0-5939-6204-6 (Hardback)

DK books are available at special discounts when purchased in bulk for sales promotions, premiums, fund-raising, or educational use.
For details, contact: DK Publishing Special Markets,
1745 Broadway, 20th Floor, New York, NY 10019
SpecialSales@dk.com

Printed and bound in China

www.dk.com
www.starwars.com

This book was made with Forest Stewardship Council™ certified paper—one small step in DK's commitment to a sustainable future. Learn more at **www.dk.com/uk/information/sustainability**

Level 1

Princess Leia's Adventures

Ruth Amos

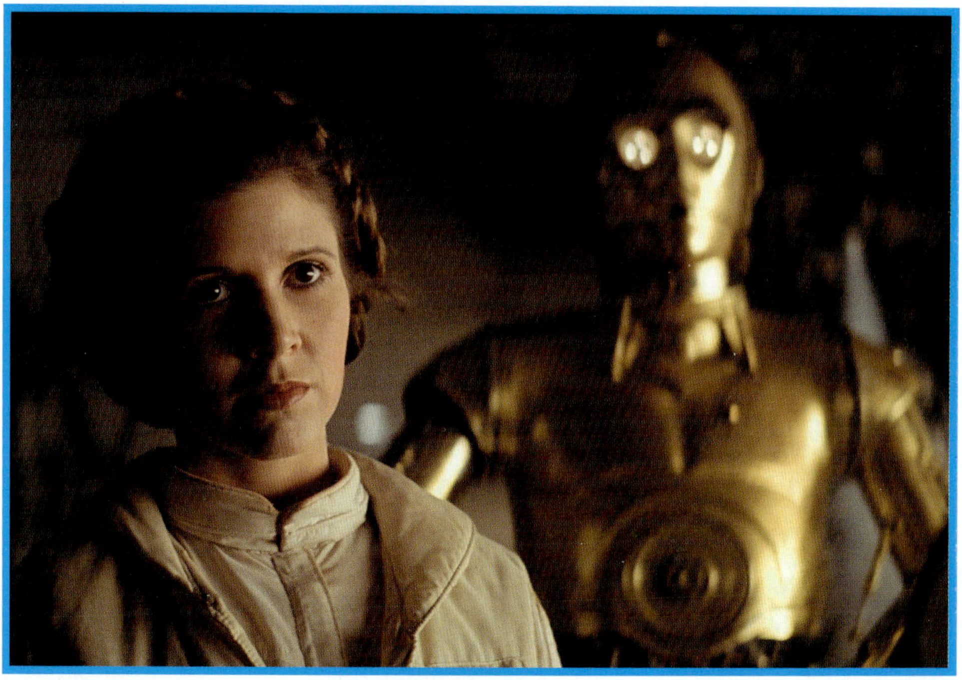

Contents

6	Meet Leia
8	Leia's family
10	Lola
12	Playtime
14	Obi-Wan Kenobi
16	The Rebel Alliance
18	Secret plans
20	Luke Skywalker
22	Chewbacca and Han Solo
24	Speeder bikes
26	The Resistance
28	Rey
30	Glossary
31	Index
32	Quiz

Meet Leia

This is Leia Organa.

Say hello to Leia!

Leia is a princess and a leader. She is very smart and brave.

Leia's family

Leia Organa's parents adopted her.
They live together on the planet Alderaan.

Leia's mother is Breha Organa. She is the queen of Alderaan.

Breha Organa

Leia's father is Bail Organa. He is a senator.

Bail Organa

Lola

Lola is Leia's droid.

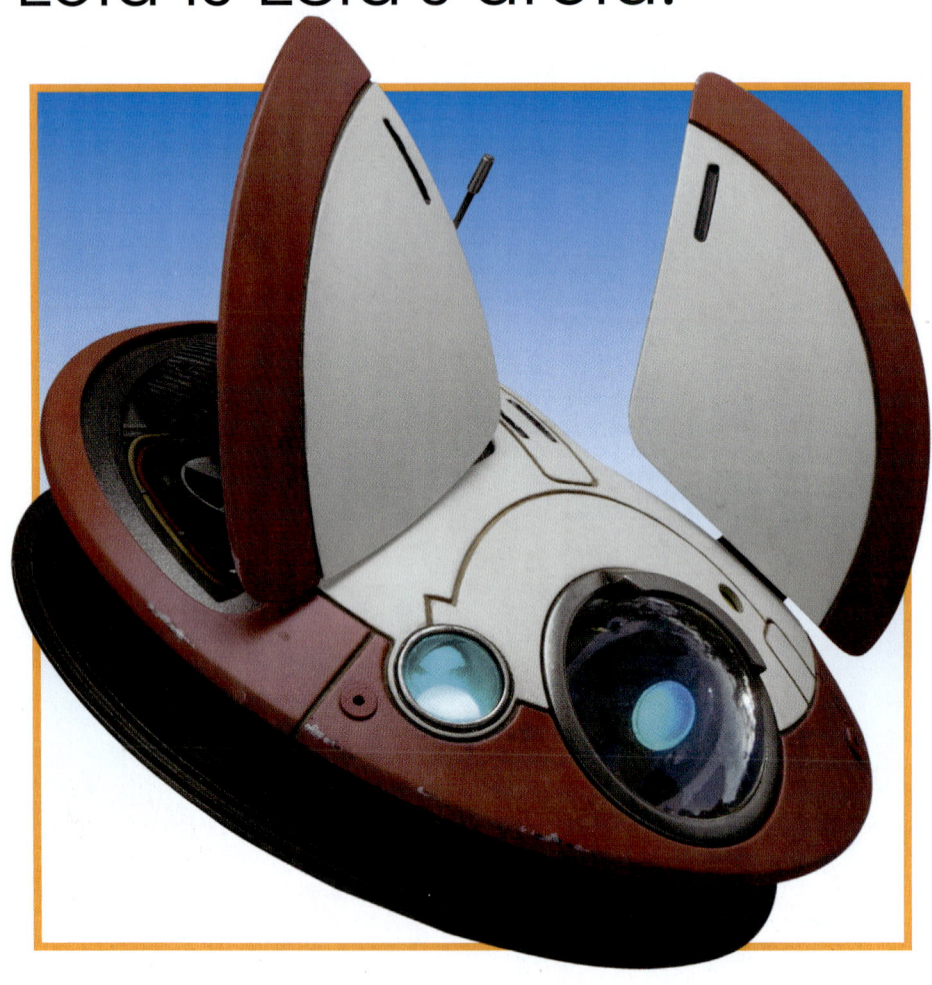

Lola's full name is LO-LA59. She can fly.

She talks to Leia by beeping.

Beep! Beep!

Playtime

Leia likes to play in the woods with Lola. Leia watches starships fly away. She likes to spot different starships.

Obi-Wan Kenobi

Leia meets a Jedi named Obi-Wan Kenobi.
A Jedi is a strong person who protects others.
Obi-Wan is kind and wise.
He helps Leia and Lola.

The Rebel Alliance

The Rebel Alliance is a group of heroes. They fight the evil Empire.

Leia joins the Alliance when she grows up. She helps battle the Empire.

Secret plans

Leia has some important plans. The Empire is trying to find them. Leia gives the plans to a droid. The droid is called R2-D2. R2-D2 will keep the plans safe.

Luke Skywalker

Luke is Leia's twin brother. He is a Jedi like Obi-Wan.

Belt

Lightsaber

Boots

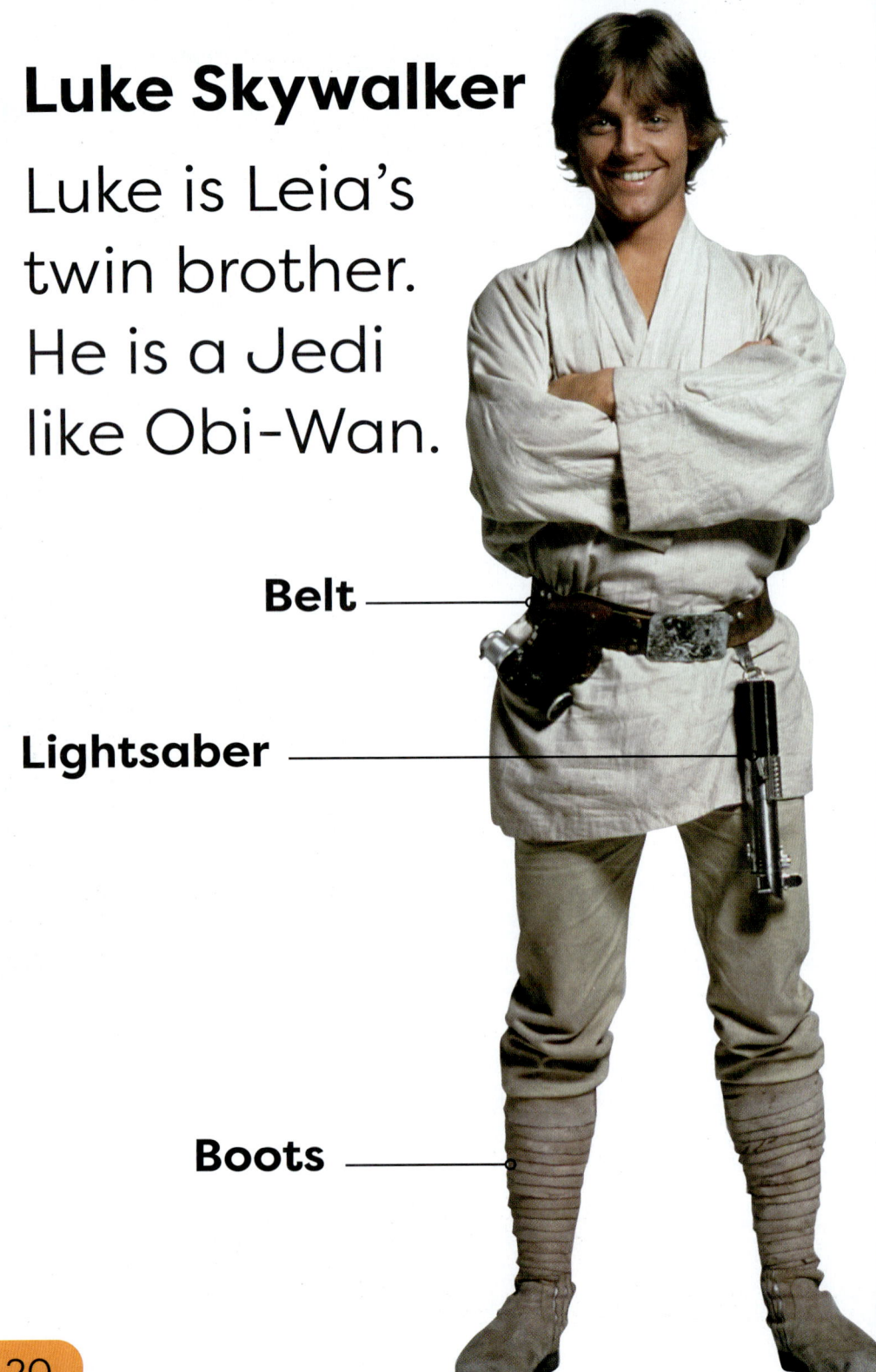

Luke teaches Leia how to be a Jedi.
He shows her how to use a lightsaber.

Chewbacca and Han Solo

Chewbacca and Han Solo are Leia's friends.
They go on adventures together in Han's starship.

The starship is called the *Millennium Falcon*.

Speeder bikes

Leia and Luke go on an adventure to the Forest Moon of Endor.
They spot some of the Empire's soldiers.

The twins chase the soldiers on speeder bikes. Leia zooms through the trees on her bike.

The Resistance

Leia sets up the Resistance group. The group fights against the First Order.

Leia

The First Order is evil like the Empire. Leia plans how the Resistance will win.

Rey

Leia meets a young woman named Rey. She teaches Rey how to be a Jedi.
Leia is a great teacher. They work together to bring peace to the galaxy.

Glossary

droid
a type of robot

lightsaber
a special sword with a long, glowing blade

senator
a person who is part of the government

speeder bike
a vehicle that hovers above the ground

starship
a vehicle that can travel through outer space

Index

Bail Organa 9
Breha Organa 9
Chewbacca 22
droid 10, 18
the Empire 16, 17, 18, 24, 27
the First Order 26, 27
Han Solo 22
Jedi 15, 20, 21, 29
lightsaber 20, 21
Luke Skywalker 20, 21, 24
Millennium Falcon 23
Obi-Wan Kenobi 15, 20
R2-D2 18

the Rebel Alliance 16, 17
the Resistance 26, 27
Rey 29
speeder bike 24, 25
starship 12, 22, 23

Quiz

Ready to find out how much you learned? Read the questions and then check your answers with an adult.

1. How does Lola talk to Leia?
2. Who does Leia give the secret plans to?
3. What is Han Solo's starship called?
4. Who does Leia chase on a speeder bike?
5. Which group does Leia set up?

1. By beeping 2. R2-D2 3. The *Millennium Falcon*
4. The Empire's soldiers 5. The Resistance